HI THIRSTY,
HI HUNGRY, I'M DAD.
HELLO BORED, I'M DAD.
HI TIRED, I'M DAD.
HI HUNGRY, I'M DAD.
HI THIRSTY, I'M DAD.
I'M DAD.
HELLO BORED, I'M DAD.
HI HUNGRY, I'M DAD.
HI TIRED, I'M DAD.
HELLO BORED, I'M DAD.
HI THIRSTY, I'M DAD.
HI TIRED, I'M DAD.
HI HUNGRY, I'M DAD.
HI THIRSTY, I'M DAD.
HELLO BORED, I'M DAD.
HI TIRED, I'M DAD.
HELLO BORED, I'M DAD.
HI THIRSTY, I'M DAD.
HI HUNGRY, I'M DAD.
HI THIRSTY, I'M DAD.
HELLO BORED, I'M DAD.
HI TIRED,

DAD MAN WALKING

For Iggy, Max & Sonya,
who make me a Dad

DAD MAN WALKING

DISPATCHES FROM THE
FRONTLINES OF FATHERHOOD
TOBY MORRIS

PENGUIN BOOKS

INTRODUCTION

Tonight, I opened my eyes realising I had dozed off on my Dad Couch. There is an empty can of beer on its arm beside me, and the highlight of my day was that when we played 'Frozen' for the I-have-lost-count-of-how-many-times time, I was finally allowed to be Elsa. A big breakthrough.

Toby gets it.

Becoming a dad is what develops during the fog of perpetual admin that is required by the title. It's something that is captured in *Dad Man Walking* in a way that's impossible not to recognise on every page. In our house, big cuddles are called 'huggles', there is currently an apple on the bench with a solitary bite out of it, and my recent in-car singing was met with a howl of two-year-old protest, followed by a voice from the back seat: 'Dad, stop, your singing is TERRIBLE!'

In this book, no doubt along with so many other dads, I feel completely seen by Toby — in a good way. Also, it's fantastic that it is mostly pictures because this dad is often far too tired to read lots of words.

Clarke Gayford, father of Neve (2)

JOURNEY TO FATHERHOOD

① THE TEST

② THE SCAN

③ THE BIRTH

④ THE FIRST PROJECTILE POOP

WHAT ARE DADS FOR?

KID-WORDS
WORDS MY KIDS USE THAT ARE BETTER THAN THE REAL ONES

CASH BROWN

SOIL MILK

GLUE-TACK

PIZZARONI
(A MAKER OF PIZZAS)

THE FIVE PHASES OF LOCKDOWN HOMESCHOOLING

① LEARNING IS EVERYTHING

② LEARNING IS EXPERIENCES

③ LEARNING IS... PLAY?

④ PLAY IS LEARNING

⑤ EVERYTHING IS LEARNING

HAS BECOMING A DAD CHANGED HOW YOU LOOK AT THE WORLD?

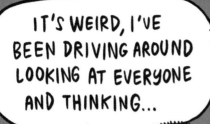

ADRIAN: THE BALLET DAD

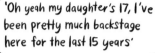

So I was like 'OK. I don't really wanna do this but I'll become a ballet dad.' I go there and I'm meeting all these other dads - like:

'Oh yeah my daughter's 17, I've been pretty much backstage here for the last 15 years'

I freaked out a bit, like 'this could be me for the next 15 years' BUT - then what I did think was cool was that this guy - his daughter's 17, and she was still running up and hugging him and kissing him in front of all her friends.

I was like... that's pretty cool. That's awesome. She obviously loves her dad.

WHAT DO DADS ACTUALLY DO?

BEGINNER DAD SKILLS:
THE 'CLIMB ON SLEEPING DAD
ON SATURDAY MORNING' GAME.

THE DEEP SATISFACTION OF A PERFECT PACK

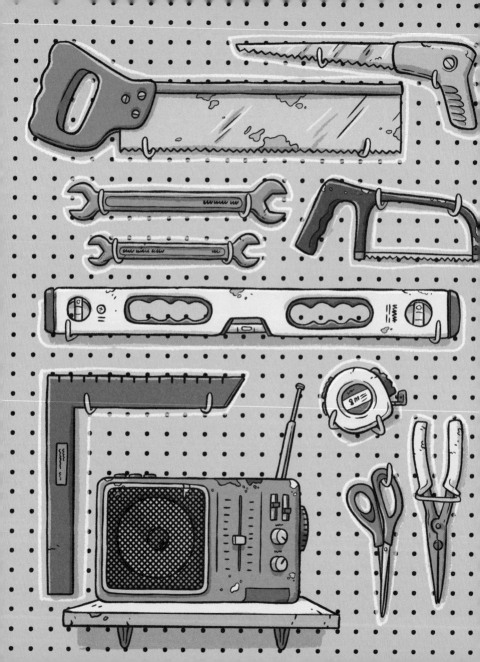

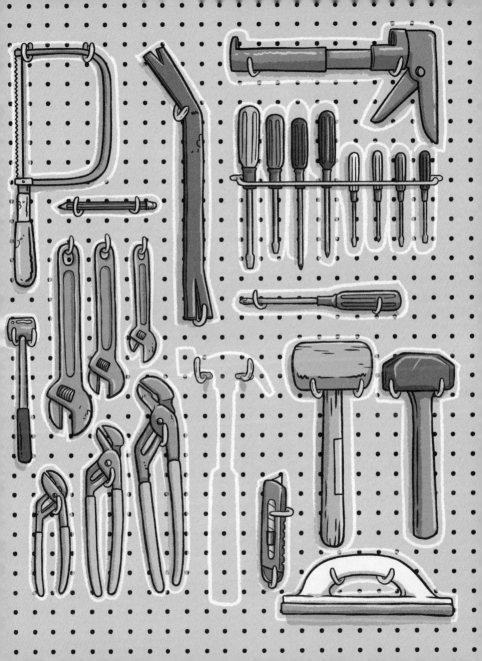

SACRED DAD OBJECT

MYSTERY GREASE

ONLY JUST STILL WORKING ELASTIC

ANCIENT PAINT

ONCE UPON A TIME SPORT WAS PLAYED IN THEM

ARE THEY 2 YEARS OLD, OR 20? WHO KNOWS?

THE WEEKEND JOB SHORTS

BRETT & DAVE

IT KEEPS GETTING BETTER—IT COMPOUNDS. YOU THINK THAT THE DAY WHERE YOUR BABY ROLLS OVER IS THE BEST DAY THAT HAS EVER HAPPENED...

FOR HER WHOLE LIFE I'VE ALWAYS FEARED THAT THE JONI I KNOW AND LOVE IS ABOUT TO BE REPLACED WITH THIS NEW VERSION...

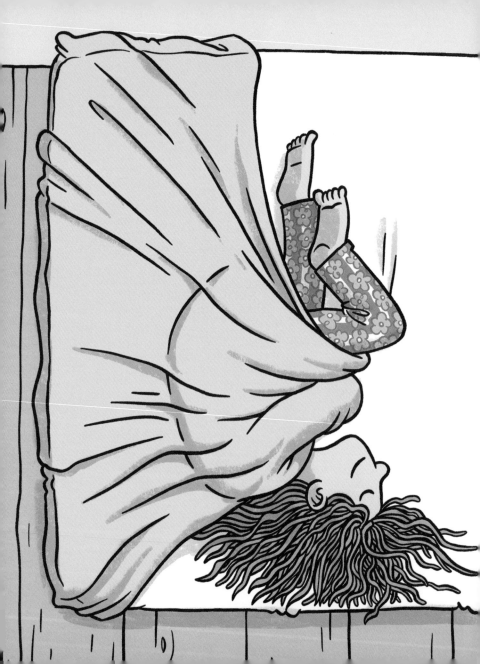

WHAT DO DADS SAY?

THE FINE ART OF INVENTING
WEEKEND JOBS THAT JUST HAPPEN
TO INVOLVE GOING PAST THE BAKERY

BEACH CRICKET
(HOW EASY DO YOU GO?)

HEY DAD, IT'S YOU...
'OH NO I'VE GOT TOO MUCH WORK TO DO'
MY HAT & SHADES
OUCH.

MORE PERFECT KID-WORDS

BABALOOMS

LIGHT
SAVER

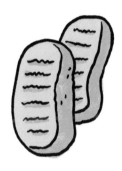

CHICKEN
MUGGETS

CONSTRUCTIONS

HOT DOCTOR

MINT
STRING

CLASSIC DADS

Sonya's dad, who wanted to boost her crawl speed

WHAT SURPRISED YOU MOST ABOUT BECOMING A DAD?

GREAT KID-WORDS III

RAINBRELLA

HAIR RINGS

SUN-SCREAM

HEARTBEEP

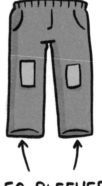

LEG SLEEVES

SCRONT

EVERY DAY

ON THE WAY TO SCHOOL

AS SOON AS WE GET TO CLASS

(IT'S COOL TO SEE THEM MAKING FRIENDS)

IS IT TRUE THAT DADS ARE ALL VERY FUNNY?

THE FIRST CUT IS THE DEEPEST

KID LOGIC

ACCORDING TO MAX AT 3YRS OLD

①

HE'S NOT ALLOWED TO EAT SPICY FOOD.

②

HE'S NOT ALLOWED TO EAT CAT FOOD.

③

THEREFORE... CAT FOOD MUST BE <u>VERY</u> SPICY.

IS THERE A MOMENT WHEN YOU'VE FELT LIKE 'THIS IS WHAT BEING A DAD IS ALL ABOUT'?

SPEED
WOBBLES

WHAT'S UP DADDY CAT?

CLASSIC DADS
Lucy's dad, whose favourite t-shirt said
MONEY & BUSINESS
ONLY

MANNERS

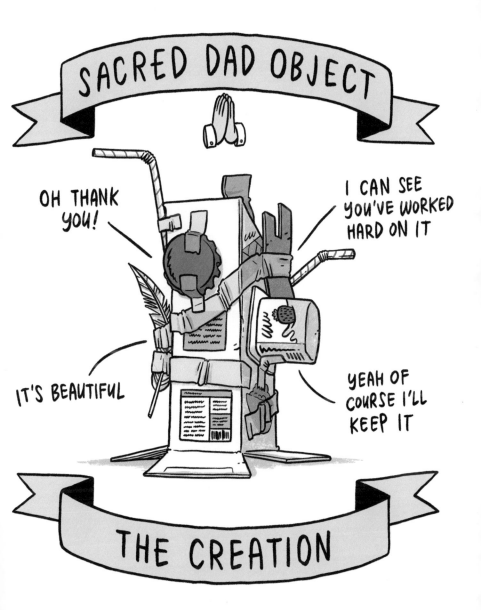

HOW CAN YOU TELL IF SOMEONE IS A DAD?

BABY SLEEP POSES: A GUIDE

BLACK PANTHER

THE DRACULA

THE MARATHON

DOWNWARD PUP

THE 'WENT DOWN FIGHTING'

WHAT IS SLEEP?

ADVANCED DAD SKILLS:
FALLING ASLEEP IN FRONT OF THE T.V.

THE CHECKLIST

Tickets booked ✓

Accommodation sorted ✓

Leave taken ✓

Bags packed ✓

Weather's perfect ✓

Gear sorted ✓

Destination reached ✓

Everyone is miserable ✓

BIG TRIP TO THE
BIG GAME.
(MOSTLY EXCITED
ABOUT HOT CHIPS)

AT THE POST OFFICE

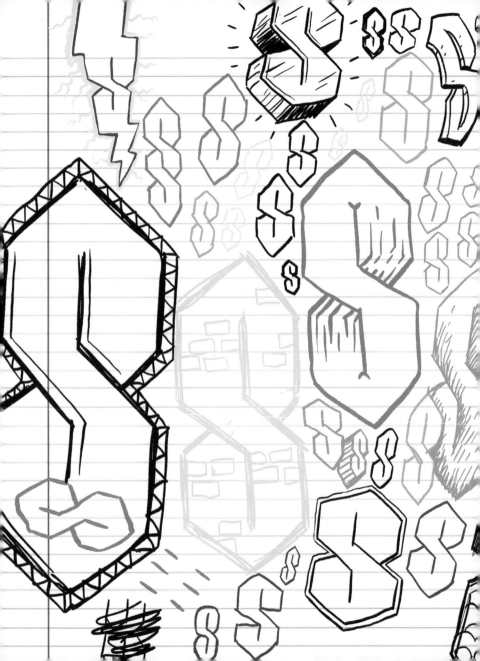

CLASSIC DADS

Paul's dad, who loved to bust out an unsolicited 'Pōkarekare Ana'

BEDTIME COMICS.
(I SECRETLY LOVE
DOING THE VOICES)

'FINISHED'

- EVERY BLOODY KID EVER.

A FEW OF THE CHARACTERS

Rhys Walbran plans on owning a motorbike, a dirt bike and a jetski by the time he's 5.

Sonya Nagels is a photographer and jeweller who is probably looking for her keys right now.

Max Morris loves spin bowling, Pokémon cards and cheese bagels with butter on them.

Simon Day is a writer, editor and podcaster. He loves cricket and cooking.

Adrian Stevanon is a television producer, Chiefs supporter and Whitney Houston fan.

Louis loves soccer, riding his bike and winding up his older brother and sister.

Iggy Morris loves rugby and making people laugh.

Eleanor Smith is a graphic designer who loves messing around with clay.

David McQuade is an emergency doctor, landslide survivor and table tennis maestro.

Brett Studholme is a full-time papa and self-described introvert, although his dance moves say otherwise.

Amba Nanu loves reading, drawing and Lego, and makes great eggs on toast.

Guy Morris is a landscaper who says every season of rugby is his last.

Hitesh Nanu is a graphic designer and marketer who has a spiritual connection with his pencil case.

Alba enjoys stealing cat food and getting tummy rubs.

Richard Key is a speech language therapist who secretly likes doing laundry.

Bonnie Williams does a convincing American accent and loves ramen.

Luke Williams is an engineer and ramen enthusiast who is plotting his future rural life.

Maeva Stevanon's favourite food is mashed potatoes and she loves to swim.

Pele Stevanon's favourite song is 'snuggle puppy', she loves to sing and her favourite food is chop suey.

Bird once led a double life with neighbours who called her Missy.

Duncan Greive is a writer and business dad. He loves reading books.

Lucy Zee is a video content creative who is devastatingly allergic to crayfish.

Mae Oliver loves singing, dancing and nachos.

Alfie Arends loves dancing and staying awake.

Paul Darragh is a Mt. Maunganui-based artist and designer that loves working in his tropical garden.

ACKNOWLEDGEMENTS

Thanks to all the dads who sat and talked with me and shared their stories and feelings - Adrian, Simon, Brett and Dave, Hitesh, Richard, Luke, Mark and Duncan. I loved talking about dad life with you all. Thanks to all the readers who've shared their stories with me that have made their way into the book too.

Thanks to my family - Sonya and Iggy and Max - for inspiration, source material and being patient with me getting your haircuts wrong. Thanks Claire, Grace, Katrina and everyone who has made turning this into a book a pleasurable experience during a tricky time.

Thanks to my own dad Andrew. Working on this has given me a new appreciation of what a positive role model of fatherhood I've had in my life. I want to acknowledge too that for lots of people dads are absent, or worse. That's a big topic for a different book, but I hear that.

To all my friends and all the kids I interviewed about how annoying and frustrating and weird dads are - I apologise for all dad jokes on behalf of all fathers around the world.

ABOUT THE AUTHOR

Toby Morris is an illustrator, cartoonist and creative director known for his non-fiction comic series *The Side Eye* and several kids' books including the comic *Te Tiriti o Waitangi*. He's drawn for bands like The Beths, Beast Wars and the Finn family, and illustrated the Edmonds baking powder box.

In 2020 his Covid-19 collaborations with Dr Siouxsie Wiles were shared around the world and he won Cartoonist of the Year at the Voyager New Zealand Media Awards.

PENGUIN

UK | USA | Canada | Ireland | Australia
India | New Zealand | South Africa | China

Penguin is an imprint of the Penguin Random House group of companies,
whose addresses can be found at global.penguinrandomhouse.com.

First published by Penguin Random House New Zealand, 2021

1 3 5 7 9 10 8 6 4 2

Text and illustrations © Toby Morris, 2021

The moral right of the author has been asserted.

Design by Katrina Duncan © Penguin Random House New Zealand
Prepress by Image Centre Group
Printed and bound in China by RR Donnelley

A catalogue record for this book is available
from the National Library of New Zealand.

ISBN 978-0-14-377517-1

MIX
Paper from
responsible sources
FSC® C144853